MW00973969

Famous Illustrated
Speeches & Documents

THE PLEDGE OF ALLEGIANCE

By Stuart A. Kallen

Illustrations by Angela Kamstra

Published by Abdo & Daughters, 4940 Viking Drive, Suite 622, Edina, Minnesota 55435.

Library bound edition distributed by Rockbottom Books, Pentagon Tower, P.O. Box 36036, Minneapolis, Minnesota 55435.

Printed in the United States.

Edited By: Julie Berg

Kallen, Stuart A., 1955-
    The Pledge of Allegiance / Stuart A. Kallen.
        p.   cm. -- (Famous Illustrated Speeches)
    Includes glossary.
    ISBN 1-56239-316-2
    1. Bellamy, Francis.   Pledge of Allegiance to the flag -- juvenile literature.
    2. Flags -- United States -- Juvenile literature.
    I. Series.
    JK1759.K25   1994
    323.6'5'0973--dc20
                                                        94-12217
                                                            CIP
                                                            AC

INTRODUCTION

The 1880s were an exciting time in the United States. New inventions such as electric lights, phonographs, telephones, and cameras were quickly changing the way millions of people lived. America had forty-four states and railroad trains criss-crossed the country.

Some of those trains delivered mail. And many children eagerly awaited the weekly delivery of their favorite magazine, *The Youth's Companion*. The Boston-based magazine was filled with tales of travel and adventure.

Children found a special project one week in 1888 when they opened up *The Youth's Companion*. The publishers asked them to raise money. The money would be used to buy United States flags for their schools. The children responded, and before long, enough pennies were collected to buy 30,000 flags.

After the success of their flag program, publishers of *The Youth's Companion* had more ideas. The year 1892 was coming soon. It would be the 400th anniversary of Columbus' voyage to the New World. *The Youth's Companion* wanted to celebrate this anniversary with something special. Two men from the magazine, Francis Bellamy and James Upham, wanted to have a nation-wide school celebration. It would be called Columbus Day. The celebration would be held on October 12, 1892, exactly four hundred years after Columbus landed in America. Children from all over the United States would raise their new flags and say something to honor the holiday.

Francis Bellamy was so excited about the holiday that he went to Washington, D.C. to tell President Benjamin Harrison. The president liked the idea so much, he made Columbus Day a national holiday. Everybody in the country, young and old, would celebrate October 12.

On a hot August night in 1892, Bellamy sat down and wrote a sentence to honor the flag. A few weeks later, children read those words in *The Youth's Companion*.

When Columbus Day finally arrived, 12 million school children recited Bellamy's salute to the flag. In Boston, 6,000 children spoke the words together while Bellamy listened. Before long, children were saying the pledge every morning in school. It became known as *The Pledge of Allegiance*.

*President Benjamin Harrison made
Columbus Day a national holiday.*

I pledge allegiance

As the pledge became more important, people argued about who had written it. The Youth's Companion said that John Upham wrote it. Francis Bellamy said that he did. In 1939, the United States Flag Association declared that Bellamy wrote the pledge. In 1957, the Library of Congress made it official.

I promise to be devoted and faithful

To the flag of the United States of America

Bellamy first wrote, "I pledge allegiance to my flag." In 1923, a committee changed the "my" to "the" and added "of the United States of America."

To the national flag of the U.S.A.

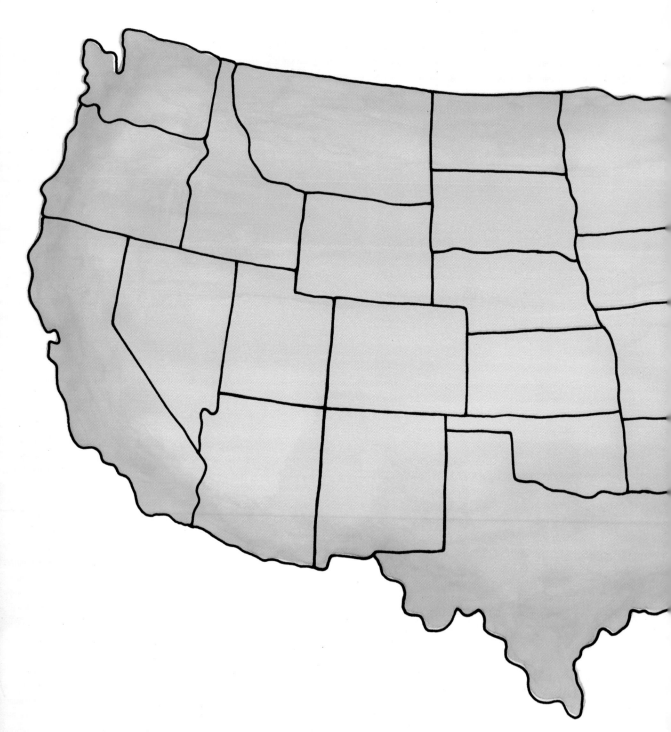

and to the Republic

A republic is a form of government where everyone can vote to elect their leaders. The United States is a republic.

and to the United States

for which it stands

In 1942, on the 50th anniversary of The Pledge of Allegiance, the U.S. Congress made it part of national law. After that, no one could change the pledge except the government.

Gazette

Sept 24 1994

that the flag represents

One nation under God,

In 1954, a congressman thought the words "under God," should be added to the pledge. Lincoln had used the words "this nation under God," in the Gettysburg Address. Congress voted to add the words. This was the last change to the pledge.

The United States is one nation joined by common bonds

indivisible,

Civil War battle scene

Thirty years before the pledge was written, the United States had been broken apart by the Civil War. When the war was over, the United States was joined together again. This made America "indivisible," or undivided.

cannot be divided or pulled apart,

with Liberty

In 1923, it was decided that people should place their right hands on their hearts when reciting The Pledge of Allegiance. A group of war veterans thought this gesture would help honor the flag.

with freedom

and Justice for all.

In 1943, the Supreme Court ruled that no person could be forced to say The Pledge of Allegiance if they did not want to.

equality under law for everyone.

FINAL WORD

In 1992, The Pledge of Allegiance celebrated its 100th birth-day. The pledge has changed over the years. And many things about the United States have changed since 1882. But one thing that has not changed: People still promise to support and love their country whenever they say the Pledge of Allegiance.

What do the colors of the American flag represent?

Red...Courage

White...Truth

Blue...Justice

THE PLEDGE OF ALLEGIANCE

I pledge allegiance to the flag

of the United States of America

and to the Republic

for which it stands,

one Nation under God,

indivisible,

with liberty and justice for all.

GLOSSARY

Allegiance - the loyalty of a person to his or her government.

Courage - mental and moral strength to venture, preserve, and withstand danger, fear, or difficulty.

Indivisible - not able to separate or divide.

Justice - equal treatment for every person.

Liberty - freedom.

Pledge - promise.

Republic - a nation where people vote for leaders to represent them.

Truth - the body of real things, events and facts.